Old Spittal and Tweed

John Griffiths

Children posed on Berwick's riverside ramparts gaze over the River Tweed, with a backdrop of Berwick Old Bridge, and Tweedmouth beyond. The bridge was built between 1610 and 1624 at a cost of £15,000. Legend has it this is because James VI & I, on crossing its dilapidated wooden predecessor in 1603 on his way to London, had stung the corporation by asking "Is there ne' a man in Berwick whae can boo [work] stanes to mak' a brig ower the Tweed?" The bridge is 1,137 feet long and 17 feet wide and has fifteen arches; the sixth pillar marked the traditional boundary between Berwick and the county palatinate of Durham, of which the Islandshire and Norhamshire districts of north Northumberland formed part. Today the bridge is still in use, although it is one way (southbound) for motor vehicles.

First published in the United Kingdom, 2011,
by Stenlake Publishing Ltd.
01290 551122
www.stenlake.co.uk
ISBN 9781840335583

The publishers regret that they cannot supply
copies of any pictures featured in this book.

Acknowledgements

The author is grateful to the staff of Berwick-upon-Tweed
Record Office and of Newcastle City Library Local Studies
Collection for their help.

Bibliography

Michael Cullen, *Later Victorian Spittal* (Berwick 2006)
John Fuller, *The History of Berwick-upon-Tweed* (1799; reprinted
    Newcastle 1973)
Stafford Linsley, *Ports and Harbours of Northumberland* (Stroud 2005)
Adam Menuge & Catherine Dewar, *Berwick-upon-Tweed. Three
    places, two nations, one town* (Swindon 2009)
Jim Walker, *History & Guide: Berwick upon Tweed* (Stroud 2001)

This three masted vessel is flying the flag of Denmark. Sailing
vessels were still a familiar site in Tweedmouth between the
wars, engaged principally in the grain and timber trades.

Introduction

Tweedmouth and Spittal are the unarguably English parts of Berwick-upon-Tweed. Unlike the medieval town of Berwick, once Scotland's premier port, and swinging between the English and Scottish crowns for two centuries before coming to rest under English control in 1482, Tweedmouth and Spittal have never been part of Scotland. But nor have they have long been part of Northumberland. Spittal and Tweedmouth were part of Islandshire, a detached portion of County Durham (known, with neighbouring Norhamshire, and Bedlingtonshire further south, collectively as 'North Durham') which was not incorporated into Northumberland until 1844. The Corporation of Berwick had bought the Manor of Tweedmouth and Spittal for £570 in 1657, to give it control of both banks of the River Tweed (and to secure useful revenues from the fisheries, coal mines and quarries of its new possession). The three settlements were formally united to create a single municipality of Berwick-upon-Tweed in 1835.

When the architectural historian Nikolaus Pevsner wrote of Berwick that it was "one of the most exciting towns in England", he was not thinking of those parts of the town south of the Tweed, and it is fair to say that most commentators have followed similar lines. Yet although largely overlooked by the tourist and the antiquarian, Tweedmouth and Spittal have long and interesting histories, which can be seen in the streets and buildings of the two settlements today.

Tweedmouth lies at the northern end of the Roman road 'the Devil's Causeway', and although no Roman remains have been discovered, it is very likely that they had an outpost of some kind here. In 1204 a castle or tower was erected in Tweedmouth - Berwick then being a Scottish port - only for it to be demolished twice by the Scottish king William I 'the Lion' (1165-1214). In 1542 'two lytel towers' are recorded in the village. Tweedmouth was to develop over the centuries as a bridgehead suburb of Berwick; like Spittal further south, its inhabitants were able to take advantage of the rich waters of the Tweed and the North Sea.

Spittal can trace its history to the thirteenth century, its name referring to the medieval leper hospital of St. Bartholomew, thought to have been located in the vicinity of Billendean Road. It developed as a fishing village, with smuggling later an important sideline, but as early as the eighteenth century it gained note locally as a health resort. The spa well on Main Street is mentioned in John Fuller's 1799 history of Berwick as being popular with visitors "particularly from the neighbourhood of Hawick. The opportunity of sea bathing at Spittal is another great inducement to persons to resort to the well." The origins of Spittal as a seaside resort and its popularity with visitors from the Scottish Borders can clearly be traced back to the influence of the spa well; while some of the problems were also to persist, for Fuller records that "in such request… is this water held, that, in the summer season, many who have come to drink it have been obliged to go home again for want of lodgings." A century or more later, local papers record how holidaymakers disappointed in the search for accommodation had to sleep on the beach.

By the late nineteenth century, when the earliest photographs in this book were taken, both Tweedmouth and Spittal were thriving industrial suburbs of Berwick. Tweedmouth had the Tweed Dock, opened in 1876 and serving not only local and visiting herring fleets but also trading in grain, stone, timber and other commodities. It was a minor railway centre, with engine sheds at Tweedmouth station, the northernmost outpost of the North Eastern Railway, and was the site of large timber works, a brewery and other trades. Spittal boasted an industrial zone around Sandstell Road, with fish curing facilities, gasworks and four artificial fertiliser factories making use of imported guano. There was also a forge specialising in spades at the south end of the village. In between were fishermen's cottages and increasing (if still inadequate) numbers of boarding houses for holidaymakers: the opening of the Kelso branch of the NER had helped Spittal to build on its existing connections with Hawick to become a major holiday resort for Borderers. In both Tweedmouth and Spittal the salmon fishery was still an important part of the local economy as well as a popular tourist 'sight'.

While Berwick 'proper' remains the cultural and commercial centre of Berwick-upon-Tweed, the centre of gravity in population terms has slipped south of the River Tweed to Tweedmouth and Spittal. In 1801, 32.5% of the total population of Berwick-upon-Tweed lived in Tweedmouth and Spittal; in 1911 the figure was 38.9%; by 1931, 43.4%; and by the 1951 census a majority of Berwick's total population of 12,554 - 6,410 or 51.1% - lived south of the river. The economic activities which allowed Tweedmouth and Spittal to grow may have dwindled, but the two settlements have become important residential districts of Berwick.

This view of Spittal, Tweedmouth and Berwick from the south dates from the 1950s. The building in the foreground, very much in use, to judge by the smoke coming from its chimney, is a 'shiel' or hut used by salmon fishermen watching out for shoals of the fish. Immediately to its right is a small Second World War pillbox.

Above: The Spa Well was already an attraction for visitors to Spittal in the eighteenth century. According to the doctor and historian John Fuller, writing in 1799, it was "a very strong spring, issuing from the face of a rising piece of Moorish ground". The water contained 'fixed air', iron and sulphuric acid, and was "beneficial in all those complaints where chalybeates and other tonics are proper to be taken… There are a great many well attested cases where it has effected a complete recovery." The signal post on the skyline indicates the presence of the Newcastle to Berwick railway line. The Spa Well and its grounds became the centre of a partially-developed 'square' with the houses of Spa Well Terrace rising up the slope to its north.

Right: This lady is using a chained cup to drink from a second well-head, probably introduced at the same time as the Spittal War Memorial, just behind the photographer, which commemorates 37 Spittal men who died in the First World War as well as those who fell in subsequent conflicts. Both well heads are now out of use.

This view neatly captures the southward expansion of what was sometimes referred to as Spittal New Town, villas and terraces for a growing middle class population and for providing holiday accommodation. Main Street here has a spacious feel: its buildings are set back from the street with long front gardens. In the centre is the iron chapel of the United Presbyterians, opened in 1887.

Marine Terrace, with the United Presbyterian chapel at the far left. The first two houses have distinctive timber watch houses above the roof line. In 1906 these were both in the possession of John Wood, and rented as apartments, as was the house next door, that of Miss Mary Ann Lillico. The tradesman standing by his horse and cart is a local greengrocer, possibly Thomas Logan of 21-23 Main Street.

Crossing Cottages still stand by the level crossing where Cow Road crosses the East Coast Main Line. Loitering on the trackside, like the couple on the far side of the line, is not recommended!

St. John's Spittal was licensed for worship in 1867 and consecrated in 1871; Spittal had previously formed part of the ecclesiastical parish of Tweedmouth. The architect may be John Howison of Newcastle, who designed St. Mary's in Berwick. The tower was added in 1894. When this photograph was taken, the incumbent was the "the idiosyncratic and controversial" Evan Rutter, the first vicar of the new parish, who remained in post until 1908 and was succeeded by the Rev. John Herbert Sutcliffe.

The immaculately clean stonework and the railings propped up against the front walls indicate this building is in the final stages of completion. The first National (Church of England) School in Spittal opened in 1873. The new school building shown here was completed in 1908, with entrances for girls (right) and infants (left) and was designed by the Berwick architects William Gray and George Boyd, who were selected after a competition. The master at the time was Thomas Borthwick (an expert violinist, known locally as 'the Paganini of the North'. He was assisted by Miss Jane Johnson and Miss Mary Noble.

This Edwardian photo exemplifies the fast-disappearing traditional fishing village of Spittal, where to use a quotation of the time "the old fashioned cottages are being replaced by better-class houses and villas." Picturesque, maybe, but in 1799 the local historian John Fuller described the houses of Spittal as being "intolerably bad, which frequently must become a source of many diseases to its inhabitants" and a century on, cottages like this were described in an 1899 report as being "on a level with the worst slums in England."

The Geisha Boys were one of the concert parties that, along with long-time favourites the Pierrots, entertained holidaymakers at Spittal.

Allars Mill was a woollen spinning mill in Jedburgh, and a major employer in the town. Their excursion to Spittal on Saturday 1st July 1911 saw employees and their families in their best clothes, and shows the popularity of the resort with Borders people. On 8th August 1913, under the headline 'Borderers Raid on Spittal' the *Berwick Advertiser* reported of "considerably over 1,000" arrivals from Galashiels, Selkirk and Hawick, noting that the accommodation available at Spittal was "quite inadequate… a few had to spend the night in the open air."

This view northwards along Main Street shows Spa Well Terrace to the left, and beyond it (with porte cochere) the flamboyant numbers 178-180 Main Street, designed circa 1850 by William Wilson, a local sculptor. To the right of the road is the iron chapel of the United Presbyterians, opened in 1887. In the distance the tower of St. John's church is visible.

Every passer-by in the neighbourhood, including a passing sailor, seems to have been rounded up by the photographer for this image of Main Street at its junction with Sea Road. St. John's church on the right is faced by the Blenheim Hotel, run by S Douglass. Nest door to it at the turn of the century was David Hardy's shop, and two doors down William Hall's confectionery shop.

The central section of Main Street, here shown looking northwards, is little changed today, closely hemmed in by rows of cottages. Many of these would have offered summer accommodation to holidaymakers. On the left at 170 Main Street is George Chisholm & Co's grocery shop.

As Main Street widens, it takes on a more commercial character, although virtually all the shop premises shown on this photograph have been converted (or re-converted) into private dwellings. On the right, the Commercial Hotel was in 1902 run by John Cavers. On the left, the view is terminated by the spire of the St Paul's Presbyterian Church. This was built in 1878, on the site of a Presbyterian Meeting House dating from 1745. The middle row of trees has been removed, but some fine specimens remain of the outer rows.

This view looking north along Main Street is taken from outside the Presbyterian Church. The flats on the right-hand side of the road were built after the Second World War to replace buildings destroyed in an air raid on 4th August 1941 in which six people died. The single-storey building at the junction with Stell Lane was a branch of Barclays' Bank circa 1930 and subsequently became the headquarters of the Berwick Salmon Co. until the company closed down in 1988. The car on the left-hand side of the road bears a Berwickshire SW registration.

In what looks suspiciously like a doctored photograph, ladies and gentlemen in their Sunday best (to say nothing of the dog) promenade on the north end of Main Street outside the Presbyterian Church. Have some been superimposed to deflect attention from the gentleman in a boater heading purposefully towards the door of the Golden Fleece Inn? In 1902 the Golden Fleece was run by James Anderson and in 1906 by Mrs. Dorothy Schirmer. By the time of this picture of circa 1912 it had passed into the hands of William Grieve. The striped pole indicates that his neighbour was a barber. A little further along, beyond the church, is the Red Lion, licensee John Hall.

Spittal Hall Farm stood on Billendean Road. For much of the early twentieth century the land was farmed by James Renton. Edward I's Hospital of St. Bartholomew, from which Spittal derives its name, is thought to have been located nearby. The farm buildings, by then disused, were deliberately burned down in 1940 during a civil defence exercise.

St. Helen's Terrace, at the northern end of Spittal Promenade, was built for the Boston family around 1897-98, and notwithstanding its proximity to the industrial area at Spittal Point became quite a fashionable street. In 1902 James Boston, of the family who controlled much of Berwick's herring trade, lived at No. 8. Other residents included the schoolmaster Charles William Hornby at No. 1, George Temple Watson at No. 2, John William Fenby at No. 4, and John Andrew Stewart at No. 6. As elsewhere in Spittal, many of the houses provided rooms for holidaymakers.

Above: The *Susan* here rests without funnel or ventilation tube, circa 1906. It may be out of commission for the winter. In the background two fishing boats can be seen mounted on trestles. In the background, the industries which developed on Spittal Point (principally artificial fertilisers, made using imported guano) are very apparent. By the early twentieth century the Point boasted a gasworks, three fertiliser factories, a vitriol and chemical works, and the Boston Brothers' fish curing establishment. Unsurprisingly, boarding house owners made frequent complaints about the smells issuing from this area.

Right: The *Susan* departs Spittal landing for Berwick, passing some of the two masted sail fishing boats of the type known as Fifies.

The *Susan*, owned by Thomas Elliott, was replaced by the *Border Chief*, built on the Clyde in 1907 and designed by the naval architect and yacht designer Cecil L'Estrange Ewen (better known as a historian of witchcraft) for the Spowart Brothers of Berwick. *Border Chief* was 40 feet long, had a beam of 10 feet and a draft of 2 feet 6 inches. It was licensed to carry 54 passengers, and had a top speed of almost 7 knots. In the river mouth a number of steam trawlers can be seen. The Spowarts went on to build up a motor bus network in the Berwick area between 1923 and 1934, when they sold out to United Automobile Services.

These clinker-built cobles by the ferry landing in Spittal were probably not always used for salmon fishing. The presence of three hat-wearing ladies on the boat to the left indicate that a pleasure trip is on the cards.

Three-masted vessels tied up at Carr Rock, Spittal. The rock, originally a natural feature, provided the deepest natural anchorage at the mouth of the Tweed and was built up into a projecting jetty under powers granted by Parliament in 1808. In the background is Berwick Pier, built 1810-21 and designed by the engineer John Rennie. Stone for the 960-yard long pier was quarried from cliffs near Spittal and brought to the riverside by horse-drawn waggonway. The lighthouse was added in 1826.

This busy scene from the mid 1960s, with beach, promenade and park all crowded with holidaymakers, catches the British seaside holiday at its postwar peak, before foreign travel became affordable for almost everybody. Dominating the picture is Forte's Venetian Pavilion of 1928, which combined café and dance hall. Forte's, still a well-known business name in Berwick, was founded by the brothers Carlo and Silviano, cousins of the hotelier Sir Charles Forte. The original 'Café' founded by the brothers, with Forte's Ices on the roof , can be seen to the rear of the Pavilion.

Spittal Promenade in the 1930s offered putting, tennis courts and a bowls green among other amusements. To the left is South Greenwich Road, named for the Greenwich Hospital, a major landowner in north Northumberland. The distant prospect is of the chimneys of the chemical factories, and the town gasometer.

Looking southwards in this view of circa 1952, another outpost of Forte's ice cream empire can be seen. A game of bowls is in full swing on the green, and the view is crowned by the cliffs of Hud's Head. That the houses here turn their backs to the sea may be due to the fact that before the promenade was made, a railway ran along bringing stone from local quarries and coal from Scremerston to the quayside and dock at Tweedmouth. The Promenade had opened in 1893, part of an attempt to provide Spittal with at least some of the facilities to be found in more sophisticated resorts. It gradually gave way to the action of the sea, and a rebuilt promenade was opened in 1998.

Most seaside resorts boasted donkey rides, but at Spittal, ponies were the norm. For many years the Spittal ponies were owned and tended by a Mr. Lieper. As well as pony rides and sea bathing, Spittal and Berwick could also provide facilities for golf, boating, angling and tennis, as well as boat trips and charabanc excurions to such places as Norham, Bamburgh, and Holy Island.

Edwardians may have enjoyed their holidays as much as later generations, but they made few concessions in the way of dress - the gentleman squatting to the right looks as if he has come straight from the office. As a contemporary guidebook noted rather worryingly that "nowhere in England can a more bracing climate be found" he may well have been grateful for his suit.

Left: These five young ladies would have been the centre of attraction in their modish beach pyjamas. These had become fashionable in 1930, the wide-legged trousers a feminised version of 'Oxford bags'. In the warm climate of the French Riviera these would normally have been worn with a sleeveless and backless blouse or swimming costume - at Spittal, warmth might have taken priority over appearance.

Below: The girls canter past the gasworks towards Sandstell Point, to the amusement of onlookers.

The salmon fishery was an important part of the economic life of Tweedmouth and Spittal; indeed, Spittal had grown up as a fishing village, with some smuggling on the side. Poaching, too, was a major problem, and between 1864 and 1884 a Royal navy gunboat was stationed at the mouth of the Tweed to aid the Tweed Bailiffs, the fishery policing authority. By the later nineteenth century the Berwick Salmon Fisheries Co. was the dominant employer, with twenty-five 'stations' on the coast and along the Tweed, working between 14th February and 14th September. On the coast, the fishermen worked in teams, as shown here, of seven or eight. A net with floats attached would be tied to a capstan on the shore, and the net paid out by two of the men rowing out to sea in a coble. One man onshore would watch for movement of the floats indicating a catch, whereupon all the men would rush to haul in the net.

The team haul their coble to the waters edge. The windlass on the right is used to help haul nets in.

A boat is pushed out to sea, with some amateur assistance.

When a possible catch was detected,
the fishermen would haul the nets in.

Nets are being carefully placed onto boats
in readiness for a further attempt.

West End, Tweedmouth is here shown as a busy community, its triangular open space flanked by houses, shops and pubs. The two pubs were the Thatched House, run in 1902 by Mrs. Rachel Heslop, and the King's Arms (the second building on the right), run by Mrs. Rachel Russell. The large castellated building behind the left-hand row of buildings is the English Presbyterian Chapel, opened in 1846; it is today occupied by Jehovah's Witnesses. In the background can be seen the parapet of the Royal Border Bridge.

Berwick's deep-water fishing fleet, largely composed of twin-masted Fifies, is here at rest in the Tweed Dock in this photo from about 1905. Fishing for herring, whose prolific numbers gained it the nickname 'the silver darling' was a staple of east coast fishing fleets for much of the nineteenth and early twentieth centuries. Overfishing, however, led to a collapse in numbers in the 1930s and the eventual demise of the industry here.

The Tweed Dock was constructed 1873-76 on land reclaimed from the foreshore, to the designs of David and Thomas Stevenson of Edinburgh (uncle and father respectively of Robert Louis Stevenson). It enclosed 3.5 acres of water and could handle vessels with a draft of 19 feet. The vessel on the right is flying the Italian flag. The white building behind the left-hand boat is The Harrow public house, whose licensee in 1906 was Samuel Stirling.

Dockside activity as sacks are loaded or unloaded from this steam vessel.

Tweed Side Albion after the 1910 season, the club was formed in 1904 and was a founding member of the Border League, alongside Coldstream, Duns, Eyemouth, Kelso, Berwick Rangers, and Percy Rovers.

The Tweedmouth Feast traditionally takes place in July. The 1913 Feast was, according to the *Berwick Advertiser* "one of the most successful in recent years" with rival funfairs creating a "horrible din" and huge crowds thronging Tweedmouth and Spittal. The sporting contests took place on Monday 22nd July, at the Pier Field in Berwick, before a large crowd, although the *Advertiser* groused that there were too many schoolboy events, with the juvenile tug of war in particular prompting a "a rush for the refreshment tent." The prizes were awarded by Miss Logan in lieu of the mayoress, and the joint secretaries of the event were D Redpath and J Crisp.

This view of Tweedmouth Station looking south-east (towards Newcastle) can be dated precisely to between 12.12 and 12.22 on Easter Sunday, 14th April 1963. The train is a five-carriage 'special' taking members of the Stephenson Locomotive Society and the Branch Line Society around southern Scotland and the Borders. The engine, number 46474, was a 2MT class 2-6-0 locomotive, the class known collectively as 'Mickey Mouse' These were designed by George Ivatt of the London Midland & Scottish Railway for light mixed traffic, and a number were also built by British Railways following Nationalisation. 46474 was built at Darlington in August 1951 and remained in service until July 1964. It was scrapped in Novemnber the same year.

Ord, or East Ord, lies a mile west of Tweedmouth. This view looks northwards across the village green, with the battlefield of Halidon Hill, north of the Tweed, on the horizon. On the right-hand edge of the photograph is Woodbine Cottage, one of a row attached to the village smithy, while the village school is situated in the centre of the green. In 1847 a report described how the master, dependent on pupils' fees for his income, would set older children to teach the younger, "a procedure which, of course, is not liked by the parents either of the older or the younger children, who say that it is the master's own business to teach, and an impropriety in him to employ the children to do his work." By the turn of the century the school had been enlarged and had an average attendance of 60 children taught by James Thompson. Half-concealed at the left-hand side of the image is the Salmon Inn, run in 1855 by William Balmer and in 1910 by Thomas Rutter.

Looking east along the main road from Coldstream to Berwick (now by-passed), this shows on the left Ord Post Office and beyond, the two-storey St. Katherine's House. The trees that close the view also conceal the grounds of Ord House.

Ord House was the ancestral home of the Ord family, who built the rearward parts of the house in the early eighteenth century. By 1789 it was owned by James Grieve, who had the front of the house built. It subsequently became the home of Francis Godolphin Osborne and remained in the Osborne family until 1954.

In 1954 Ord House and Park were bought by George Marshall, manager of the Berwick branch of the Walter Wilson grocery chain, and two associates. Marshall became sole owner by 1956, and recreated the estate as a holiday park. After he died in 1991, the park was run by his son Howard Marshall and in 2003 it was sold to Billy Maguire. Ord House now houses a bar-restaurant and other facilities and a shop has been built on to one side, while the park offers holiday homes as well as touring caravan pitches.

This view of Richardson's Stead looking northwards reminds us that Scremerston was more than a pit village, and lies in a belt of rich farming country, described by Walter White in 1859 as the "the best part of the country for wheat". In 1873 the *Newcastle Weekly Chronicle* described the pitmen' cottages of Richardson's Stead as forming a square, "in the centre of which stands a huge ash heap, flanked by a few almost roofless coal-houses… general appearance of the place is squalid in the extreme." The farm, which is almost certainly Middle Scremerston, was cultivated in 1910 by the Ross Brothers and stood on the Great North Road in the centre of what is now Scremerston village, the site occupied today by Prince Charles Place. The parish church is situated just over the brow of the hill on the right, and just visible is the schoolmaster's house (John Wright in 1910).

The female field workers shown here were called 'bondagers' who were engaged by male farm-workers (known in northeast England and the Scottish Lowlands as 'hinds') to work for them for one year. This system dated back to the seventeenth century, and persisted until after the First World War in some districts near Berwick. Sometimes a bondager might be a hind's daughter; otherwise, unmarried women would be chosen, at annual 'hiring fairs' One Victorian account described bondagers as "girls of loose character and lost reputation", perhaps because they had to share the hind's cottage. Other reports, however, attest to their good character. As shown in this picture, bondagers wore a characteristic costume of skirt, apron, print blouse, pink neckerchief and a voluminous bonnet of varnished straw, which protected them from the sun and from inclement weather.

Scremerston from the north. Barely visible behind the trees on the left is the Miners' Arms public house, just inside the Berwick borough boundary and run in 1921 by Mrs. Janet Cuthbert. In the distance is the spire of St. Peter's Church, of 1842-3, deigned by Ignatius Bonomi and John Augustus Cory. To the right of the Great North Road, the pithead gear and engine house of Scremerston Colliery are largely hidden by a pit heap. The long straight of the road was an irresistible attraction for early motorists, and Scremerston had more than its share of road accidents.

Allerdean Colliery was a small coal mine located three miles south of Berwick. It was abandoned in 1965, at which time nine surface and twelve underground workers lost their jobs.

Sea House, Scremerston was the home, until his death in 1894, of Thomas Johnson, chairman of the Scremerston Coal Company (the Johnson family were recorded as owners of the mine as early as the 1820s). In 1921 it was home to Frederick Whiteside and by 1928 was being run by the Whitesides as a private hotel. In 1938 this was in the hands of Miss J D Bradford, and was put up for sale in 1939 before being requisitioned for military use.

Scremerston Railway Station on the North Eastern Railway's main line between Berwick and Newcastle was opened, along with the Tweedmouth to Chathill section of the line, on 29th March 1847. It was probably designed by Benjamin Green, who, with his father John, was responsible for Grey's Monument and the Theatre Royal in Newcastle. The stationmaster in the mid 1890s was Robert Heir. The station closed to passengers on 8th July 1951 and is now a private house.

Scremerston lies at the northern tip of the Great North Coalfield, and its colliery was a major employer in the village. At the time of this photo it was run by the Scremerston Coal Company, whose manager was J Evelyn Carr, and employed around 200 to 300 men in various pits in the district. Shown here is the Restoration Pit. After years of uncertainty the mine closed briefly in 1935 after the failure of the coal company, but resumed work under new ownership until final closure in the mid 1940s. Derwentwater Terrace was named after the Earls of Derwentwater, traditional manorial lords of Scremerston. After the attainder and execution of the third earl for his part in the 1715 Jacobite rebellion, his lands were granted to the Greenwich Hospital.

Haggerston Castle was built around the medieval tower of the Haggerston family, successively rebuilt and enlarged by them in the 1770s and 1808-11. In the mid-nineteenth century it was sold by the family, and in 1893 Christopher Leyland commissioned the architect Norman Shaw to further enlarge and embellish the building. Shaw designed the rotunda entrance hall and the castellated, 153 feet high water tower (which also included an observatory) as well as building three new wings to the house. The resulting "Victorian white elephant" was badly damaged in a fire of 1911 and remodelled by James B Dunn of Edinburgh. The completed building boasted nine reception rooms (including a ballroom and winter garden), 29 bedrooms, two nurseries, twelve marble-lined bathrooms, and twelve staff bedrooms. However, after Leyland's death in 1923, the estate, including 1750 acres and the village of Fenwick, was sold by his son in 1930-31 and the house largely demolished. The rotunda and water tower alone remain, dominating a holiday camp developed in its grounds.

Haggerston was at the centre of a kidnapping saga in 1905-06. Leyland was the guardian of the two daughters of Florence Chetwynd, a distant relative (and, scandalously for that time, a divorcee), who sought to regain custody of her children. To that end she paid £500 to a Thomas Duguid and his lady friend Esther Quayle. They befriended Leyland's housekeeper with a view to kidnapping the girls, aged 13 and 15, while out walking with their governess, and taking them by yacht or hired steamer to San Sebastian in northern Spain. The plot was revealed and Duguid was sentenced to nine months imprisonment, but Quayle was acquitted.

Leyland kept a private zoo of exotic species at Haggerston which included black buck antelope, kangaroos, and Europe's largest herd of North American bison. He was also a keen horticulturalist, participating in the development of the fast-growing hybrid evergreen *Leylandii* at Haggerston; and he was a crewman on the *Turbinia*, the world's first turbine-powered boat.